What's Next?

A guide to dealing with grief after a loss

Written by Tamar Knibye

Keisha Sando

What's Next?

Printed by CreateSpace, An Amazon.com Company

©2015

The strategies outlined in this pamphlet are options that a mother, father, or children can use to heal. They are not to be construed as the only ideas a person can use.

Keep in mind every person is different and handles grief in his or her own unique way. We progress in stages with plateaus and developmental crisis that demand change (Nichols, 1999).
We pray that you will find peace and that one of these strategies will help you begin your healing process.

Table of Contents

Understanding the Psychological Components of Grief

It is important to recognize that the next step will differ depending upon one's history, culture, religious affiliation, etc. Western society tends to view bereavement as an interference in the daily routine of life, troublesome, and a debilitating emotional response that one must overcome as quickly and efficiently as possible (Comer, 2001). Some individuals may find support from their family and friends, while some may not appear to have been affected by losing a child. Losing a baby is considered a traumatic event and facing any type of trauma can affect someone physically, emotionally, as well as spiritually.

Elisabeth Kübler-Ross developed the concept of what is known as Kübler-Ross' Five Stages of Grief (Vander Zanden, 2003). These stages of grief were based on her studies of the feelings of patients facing a terminal illness, but many people have generalized them to other types of negative life changes and losses, such as the death of a loved one or a breakup (Smith and Segal, 2014 Help Guide).

While some people will move through the stages in order, this will not be the case for everyone. Some may only be able to move through two out of the five stages. Not everyone goes through all of the stages; some slip back and forth between stages, and some experience several stages at the same time (Vander Zanden, 2003). Not everyone has to go through the stages to heal. For many people, recovery after bereavement takes 18 to 24 months, but for others, the grieving process may be either longer or shorter (Segal and Smith, 2014).

As you read through the stages of grief, you will also find an explanation of some women's experiences during those stages.

Think about the stage and ask yourself some questions. Where do you see yourself? Did you have similar feelings? Do you feel as if you are in that stage, past that stage, or did not go through the stage at all?

The First Stage of Grief: Denial/Isolation

Entailed in this stage is one's struggle with acknowledging and/or dealing with reality. During this stage, the mother or father may immediately deny the fact that they really lost their child when they first receive the news. This is a normal response and is actually the way the mind defends itself from being tremendously affected by a traumatic experience. Losing a baby can cause a mom or parent to feel numb. A mom or dad may not cry or sometimes may not even speak for days, weeks, or on some occasions, months, about what happened. They feel empty, they continue to avoid social relationships, and their loss increases (Comer, 2001).

The Second Stage of Grief: Anger

During this phase, a mother, father or sibling may become irritable, short in conversation, and/or verbally or physically aggressive. They might look at the persons around them and feel envy, jealousy, and rage over their health and vigor (Vander Zanden, 2003). Some individuals are angry with the unborn child. We may resent the person for causing us pain or for leaving us (Axelrod, 2006).

The Third Stage of Grief: Bargaining

In this phase, individuals are trying to regain control over their lives. It's a vain expression of hope that the bad news is reversible. Secretly, we may make a deal with God or our higher power in an attempt to postpone the inevitable (Axelrod, 2006). Parents may start to question themselves and the decisions that they made prior to losing their baby. Statements and/or thoughts may start off with "If I only had . . .", "They should have . . .", or "I should have known . . ." In this stage, one may be fixated on what happened and may find themselves constantly searching for answers regarding the loss of the baby. While this is a normal response, staying in this stage may prevent someone from living a fulfilled life.

The Fourth Stage of Grief:
Depression

Anger can often be a sign that someone is depressed. Sadness and regret predominate this type of depression. It is our quiet preparation to separate and to bid our loved one farewell (Axelrod, 2006). A parent may feel like he or she has lost motivation and may possess no desire to continue on with daily activities during the stage of depression, or may lose the desire to spend time with his or her friends, especially those that have children or somehow remind them of their baby. During this stage, one may also blame himself or others for what happened. A parent may also continue to replay words or specific scenarios surrounding the incident, which can contribute to the cycle of depression.

The Fifth Stage of Grief: Acceptance

In the Acceptance stage, they no longer struggle against death (in this case, that of their child), but make peace with it (Vander Zanden, 2003). It is during this phase that parents recognize that they have to continue on and adjust their minds and lives, to change from what they were expecting. When someone has begun to accept their loss, this does not mean that they are fine with losing their child, but they realize that they will have to continue on without the physical being of their child.

Perspectives

The stages of grief can look different for each one of you based on the time of the loss, your environment, or how you process the grief. As we continue, you will take a look at how various women have moved through each stage differently.

Denial/Isolation

Denial/Isolation from a First Trimester loss perspective:

I went to get a sonogram about a week after finding out I was pregnant. I had finally come to terms with the idea of having two babies at home. I was becoming happy with the benefits of having two children close in age. After waiting several moments while the technician was looking at my uterus, they told me that the embryo was 9 weeks old and there was no heartbeat. I recall feeling numb. I had put myself through an emotional roller coaster, then I was being told that I was no longer pregnant. I began to question whether or not I really was pregnant, especially since I didn't feel like it anyway.

Denial/Isolation from a Second Trimester loss perspective:

This was an interesting stage for me because I can still remember that day when the doctor told me my baby had died. I could not believe that he was telling me something like that. I had heard about it happening to others, a friend of the family, one of the staff at my college, but who could imagine that it would happen to me. I cried right away, though; so much information at one time and I could not handle it all. Right then, there was an emptiness that I could not explain.

It was a while before my husband and I really talked about it. For the first week, unless I was going to the doctor, I hung around the house and did not talk to anyone unless they called and asked questions.

As far as my husband and I discussing the situation, I can not remember when we started talking about it, but I do know that weeks went by before we did. There are moments and times when you do not know what to say or how to approach a difficult situation. I did not know what to say to him, and he did not know what to say to me.

Denial/Isolation from a Post-Birth perspective:

It is hard to deny the fact that Eleanora was gone when her absence was present everywhere we looked. Her room was filled with all of her clothes waiting to be worn, toys to be played with, and other things that go along with a baby. Her bassinet where she laid her beautiful head just the night before was now painfully and deafeningly empty. It was hard to deny that she was gone when her cooing no longer woke me up at night to nurse. The heaviness of my empty arms reminded me that she was no longer here.

However, when they were doing CPR to bring her back to us I kept asking if she would be okay. "Surely, they could bring her back", I thought, against all reason. I was just holding a happy, healthy baby one minute, and what felt like the next minute, doctors were fighting for her next breath. It all happened in an instant.

While we were in the emergency room watching the group of doctors and nurses work to save her, I prayed over and over to please let her live, begging God not to take her away from us. I pleaded with God for a miracle. Leaving my precious baby girl alone in the hospital emergency room was one of the hardest things I have ever had to do. It was hard to deny that she was gone at that point. (Natalie Scott, personal communication, May 16, 2016)

Anger

Anger from a Second Trimester loss perspective:

I did enter this phase for a short period of time. My anger was geared more toward the doctor who gave me the news about the baby. Number one, I felt like he was very cold and unemotional when he was talking to me. Then, he insinuated that I should have known something when the symptoms stopped. Well, how was I supposed to know? this was my first pregnancy, so I thought symptoms were supposed to stop at some point. I felt like he was blaming me for not figuring it out a week or two sooner. How could he?

I did not lash out at anyone, though. By nature, I am introverted, so my battles were more internal. I did not express anger toward a particular person; I mostly kept it to myself.

Anger from a Post-Birth perspective.

I was never angry with Eleanora. In my mind, she did not want to leave. I have gone through several stages of anger. I go in and out of this stage, still, five years later. At the beginning, I was angry at every mother who had a baby, after Eleanora passed away, and got to keep her baby. I was, and still am, jealous of every first time mom who naively has and keeps her baby, which is what I was. Since I lost a girl and then later had two boys, this stage of anger/jealousy is a constant ebb and flow in my life, as I watch other little girls grow up. I will never know what my little girl would have been like. That thought will cause me to slip into the stage of depression. (Natalie Scott, personal communication, May 15, 2016)

Bargaining

Bargaining from a First Trimester loss perspective:

Within days, I began to blame myself for losing the fetus. I told myself that I was so physically and emotionally stressed that my body could not contain the fetus. I had asked the doctor why it happened, but was simply told that there was no identified reason. In fact, the doctor explained that many women experience miscarriages in the first trimester and normally attribute it to a late period.

Bargaining from a Second Trimester perspective:

I remember when I had to go to the doctor a couple of days after the news of losing my baby. The doctor said she was going to do another ultrasound to check everything out. My hope was kindled because I believed that she was going to look on that ultrasound and see that my baby started breathing again and that I did not have to have surgery.

As far fetched as that was, I believed it could happen. That was my only option at that point because I felt like I had made the necessary precautions to keep my baby safe. Once during my pregnancy when I had a chance to go bowling, I decided not to because I did not want to hurt myself or the baby. I was not doing anything to overexert myself or anything that I would question myself about later.

Bargaining from a Post-Birth perspective:

I spent many sleepless nights for years, focused on what, in my mind, I did wrong. "If I would have done this...I should have done that...", I go over every detail of the morning she passed away. I beat up myself mentally. In moments of clarity, I know there was nothing more that could have been done, but when I am trapped in the clutches of these evil thoughts, I cannot see past my perceived faults.

My way of tamping down these negative thoughts were to constantly have noise, music or television, to distract my mind from reliving the same painful moments over and over. Family, friends, even doctors and one close friend who said just the right words, assured me there was nothing more that could have been done and I am more confident that I did everything I could have done. Now, I only occasionally find myself questioning the events of that day. (Natalie Scott, personal communication, May 15, 2016)

Depression

Depression from a Second Trimester perspective:

Depression did not last long for me. There was a specific event that happened that caused me to be temporarily depressed. I found out my baby died on December 1, 2008, and then I found out my sister was pregnant on December 31, 2008. I was hurt and angry and felt sorry for myself. I remember her calling and telling me I was going to be an aunt. The phone conversation continued for maybe another couple of minutes, but from that point on it was over for me. I gave the phone to my husband because I was on the verge of bursting into tears.

Here I was, had just lost my baby and my sister was about to have one. I was happy for her, of course, but was angry with her for telling me so soon. I cried and cried and cried. I felt sorry for myself for hours after that. I could not look the next person in the eye without crying. I did not want to talk to anyone, see anyone, or be around anyone. Nevertheless, I purposefully did not shut myself off from others. After that day, I decided to just be happy for her and throw myself into helping prepare for the baby. After all, she did not plan on being pregnant around that time, and I know it was a hard decision for her to tell me the news to begin with. What I didn't want was her to stress over how I was feeling about the whole thing and give her any unnecessary stress. She was my sister and I needed to support her, no matter what. "

Depression from a Post-Birth perspective:

Anger/jealousy, bargaining/ questioning myself and depression were my constant companions. While I no longer had my baby to hold, I was encircled with these constant emotions sending me up and down a roller coaster for years. I believe the grieving process can take a lifetime until we are reunited with our babies in heaven. I continue to slip in and out of this stage, as I watch little girls grow up. It was hard for me to even watch my second child achieve milestones that my daughter never had a chance to achieve. At the beginning, I avoided

any pregnant mother, baby showers, baby stores and anything to do with babies. I didn't go to celebrations at work as a way to avoid a pregnant coworker. To me, it felt like their swelling bellies were mocking me. I closed my office door and avoided happy chatter about the upcoming baby and subsequent delivery. No one understood my misery. It was a very lonely and isolating time for me."
(Natalie Scott, personal communication, May 15, 2016)

Acceptance

Acceptance from a First Trimester loss perspective

My oldest child is eight years older than my 10 month old baby, and I certainly wonder what life would have been like if that baby would have been born. I wonder if it would have been a boy or girl. My oldest son is a very friendly child and wishes he had siblings around his age. I sometimes feel like his desire could have been a reality if I did not have a miscarriage. I know that it is not beneficial for me to dwell on the "what if?". Instead, I embrace the close relationship that I was able to establish with my son because he was the only child for so long. I have learned that in life we will have challenges, surprises and adjustments, but we have to make the most out of what is given and when it is given.

Acceptance from a Second Trimester loss perspective

I did accept the truth that I had a baby. But it did not end there. I had to also accept that I had not lost one, but two babies. Just two months after my first baby died, I got pregnant again, but it turned out to be an ectopic pregnancy. Some might question that in an ectopic pregnancy whether or not it was a baby at all, or just a zygote. I believe that from the time the egg is fertilized, that it is a baby no matter how small it starts off. There were now two failed pregnancies in my life, but I could not lose hope and stop there. Whether we were going to have our own child or adopt, we had to move forward with our lives. The world had not stopped spinning, and life was still happening all around. My goal was to live it and know that there was something in store for me. I had a desire, and that was to be a mom.

Acceptance from a Post-Birth perspective.

I am not sure when I reached this stage, but, for me, acceptance meant celebrating her life. We celebrate her birthday every year and find other ways to remember her and keep her memory alive. We talk about her with our other kids. We talk about how she is still with us in our hearts and guiding us. When people ask how many kids I have I include her. Although I have accepted she is not here on earth, talking about and including her helps me. Acceptance, for me, is every day. Every day I have to acknowledge that I have to go on without her. I carry her memories in my heart, so I know she is never far away." (Natalie Scott, personal communication, May 15, 2016)

Strategies for Dealing with Grief

Grief is something that does not just go away on its own. Yes, everyone experiences it in his or her own way, but, most times, action needs to be taken to get past the constant hurt. Below, you will find practical strategies for dealing with grief, and in the long run, become free from the potential lasting effects of it.

- Positive Self-Talk Example: "I can be a great parent." "I am not alone. I have the support of many people around me." "I play an important role in my family." "I am a happy person." "I can laugh again."

- Some individuals will need to see a therapist who can help them work through their hurt, pain, and confusion.

- It is advisable to find someone who is trustworthy and willing to listen. Sometimes a person just needs to let it all out. Open your heart and express what is there.

- It is important to work towards labeling the specific feelings that one may be feeling, including anger, guilt, anxiety and/or sadness.

- During this time, it is crucial to be careful not to make any major changes in your life. If it is inevitable, it is best to be extremely thoughtful about the decision and consult others.

- Closure can be encouraged with a ceremony for the baby, which can also be held on the anniversary.

- Sometimes people have difficulties with expressing themselves verbally. Creating an art project as a tribute to the baby is another useful way of expression. It's honoring the baby as well as expressing one's thoughts and feelings in a healthy manner that is at their own pace. One example is to create a collage.

- During the Bargaining stage, it is especially important not to allow those irrational thoughts to fill your mind, for example, having the thought of "I should have done _____ sooner."

- Make a list of people that are close to you that you can reach out to when you need to; even if it is just to listen.

- Write a letter to the lost child

- Write in a journal

- Exercise, which boosts the mood

- Ask questions from the doctor of other options, explanations, etc., regarding the reasons for the loss of the child

- If there are other family members involved (i.e. siblings), have them make a special card for the child.

- Siblings can also write letters to their parents expressing their love for mom and dad and encourage their parents

- Numerous self-help bereavement groups allow mourners opportunities to gather with others who have lost loved ones, to discuss the emotional and practical problems they all face (Comer, 2001).

Additional Strategies

These, by far, are not the only options that can be used to help with healing. I (Tamar Knibye) took a more spiritual approach and decided to make confessions for myself. I took scriptures right from the Bible, and I personalized them. Because God is the same God yesterday, today, and forever, anything He said about a woman and her womb could still apply to me.

I spoke those things that had not manifested yet as though they had. These were not just for during the pregnancy. I confessed them before I became pregnant again, too. I had to believe what I was saying. I had to have faith. Here are some of the confessions that I quoted on a regular basis to help build my faith and keep my hope alive.

<u>Confessions</u>

"Behold, children are a heritage from the LORD, The fruit of the womb is a reward." (Psalm 127:3, NKJV)

"By the God of your father who will help you, And by the Almighty who will bless you With blessings of Heaven above, Blessings of the deep that lies beneath, Blessings of the breasts and of the womb."(Genesis 49:25, NKJV)

"Then she spoke out with a loud voice and said, 'Blessed are you among women, and blessed is the fruit of your womb!'" (Luke 1:42, NKJV)

"And He will love you and bless you and multiply you; He will also bless the fruit of your womb and the fruit of your land, your grain and your new wine and your oil, the increase of your cattle and the offspring of your flock, in the land of which He swore to your fathers to give you. "(Deuteronomy 7:13, NKJV)

"Blessing I will bless you, and multiplying I will multiply your descendants as the stars of the heaven and as the sand which is on the seashore; and your descendants shall possess the gate of their enemies. "(Genesis 22:17, NKJV)

"For he will be great in the sight of the Lord, and shall drink neither wine nor strong drink. He will also be filled with the Holy Spirit, even from his mother's womb." (Luke 1:15, NKJV)

"In your seed all the nations of the earth shall be blessed, because you have obeyed My voice." (Genesis 22:18, NKJV)

"Then God blessed them, and God said to them, 'Be fruitful and multiply; fill the earth and subdue it; have dominion over the fish of the sea, over the birds of the air, and over every living thing that moves on the earth.'" (Genesis 1:28, NKJV)

"I will make you exceedingly fruitful; and I will make nations of you, and kings shall come from you." (Genesis 17:6, NKJV)

"May God Almighty bless you, And make you fruitful and multiply you, That you may be an assembly of peoples;" (Genesis 28:3, NKJV)

"Also God said to him: 'I am God Almighty. Be fruitful and multiply; a nation and a company of nations shall proceed from you, and kings shall come from your body.'" (Genesis 35:11, NKJV)

"For I will look on you favorably and make you fruitful, multiply you and confirm My covenant with you." (Leviticus 26:9, NKJV)

"25 Strength and honor are her clothing;

She shall rejoice in time to come.

26 She opens her mouth with wisdom,

And on her tongue is the law of kindness.

27 She watches over the ways of her

household, And does not eat the bread of

idleness.

28 Her children rise up and call her blessed;

Her husband also, and he praises her:

29 Many daughters have done well,

But you excel them all." (Proverbs 31:25-29,
NKJV)

My hope and expectation is that you start to heal as I have. It is your day to be free from the hurt that plagues your mind, monthly, weekly, and even daily. I want you to understand that, "You do heal, but you're never the same" (Courageous, 2011). Loss takes something from you and out of you, but it should not be the end. IT IS NOT THE END!

If you would like to hear more of my personal story of loss, pick up "Letting Go of Baby: A story of never-ending faith after the heartbreak of miscarriage", available on Amazon.com and digitally on Kindle.

Resources

If you are in the Brooklyn, New York area and are looking for a counselor, you can contact Peace-Filled Mental Health Counseling Services (PFCS). For contact information go to https://www.peacefilledcs.com and https://www.facebook.com/peacefilledcs

There are also websites that you can go to, to find a counselor in your area:

- www.psychologytoday.com
- www.therapysites.com
- www.apa.org
- www.goodtherapy.org

References

For additional information, references for the information given in this pamphlet are below.

Axelrod, J. (2006). The 5 Stages of Loss and Grief. Psych Central. Retrieved on February 24, 2015, from http://psychcentral.com/lib/the-5-stages-of-loss-and-grief/000617

Smith, M and Segal, J. (2014) Supporting a grieving person. Retrieved on February 22, 2014 from www.helpguide.org

Smith, M and Segal, J. (2014) Coping with Grief and Loss. Retrieved on February 23, 2014 from www.helpguide.org

Comer, R. J. (2001) Abnormal Psychology (4th ed). New York, New York: Catherine Woods

Crandell, T. L., Crandell, C. H. & Vander Zanden, J. W. (2003) Human Development (7th ed.) (Rev. ed) New York, NY: McGraw Hill.

Nichols, M. P. (1999) Inside Family Therapy; A Case Study In Family Healing Needham Heights, MA: Allyn & Bacon

Kendrick, A. (Director), Catt, M., Hemmings, T. & McBride, J. (Executive Producers). (2011). *Courageous*. [Film]. United States: TriStar Pictures.

About the Authors

Keisha Jeannine Sando is a Licensed Mental Health Counselor (LMHC). She received her Masters in Counseling Psychology from Bowie State University and her Bachelor's degree in Psychology from Eastern University. She has been in the counseling field for 14 years and has obtained a great deal of experience, specializing in various fields of Mental Health. Keisha is the founder and director of Peace-Filled Mental Health Counseling Services where she and her therapist provide counseling to children, adults, families and couples. Keisha also serves as director for a counseling center named Zoe Center for Growth, which is organized at Hope Christian Center, a church in Brooklyn, NY.

Keisha enjoys working with organizations and individuals to provide assistance with developing counseling programs. She has a heart and passion for helping individuals develop coping skills, regain strength, work through their trauma and obtain emotional wellness. She has also helped individuals learn the skills to manage their anger, reduce stress and build self-confidence.

In her leisure, Keisha enjoys listening to music, singing and spending time with friends and her husband and two boys. She goes by the motto, "Change your perspective; change your life." She believes that it is not simply your experience that shapes your life but how you perceive what you are going through as well as your motivation to get through it that determines your future.

Tamar Monique Knibye is a certified teacher in the Brandywine School District. Tamar received her Bachelor's degree in Education from Eastern University and is certified K-6. She has taught Kindergarten for the past 12 years. When in the classroom, her desire is to give children the foundations they need to be able to read by the end of Kindergarten, if not before then, and to make sure that learning continues to be fun for our children.

In December 2014, Tamar became the author of her first self-published book, *Letting Go of Baby*. The book came about as a result of the loss of her unborn child in 2008 and ectopic pregnancy in 2009. *Letting Go of Baby* depicts her story of the circumstances that lead up to the loss of her baby and the events thereafter. Tamar's purpose of the book was a desire to see that no woman goes

53

through the loss of a child alone. She wanted to help other women get through the heartache and pain and still be able to live life with hope.

In her leisure, Tamar enjoys time with her family, music, dancing, and recreational activities. Tamar is married to Tsombawi Knibye, Jr., and has two children; a son, Tsombawi Knibye III, and a daughter, Kadesh Knibye. Her favorite verse from the bible is Psalm 34:19: "Many are the afflictions of the righteous: but the Lord delivereth him out of them all." She believes that no matter what situation you are in, God is there to constantly bring you out.

To contact me I can be emailed at Tamarknibye@groups.facebook.com.

To access my website go to www.facebook.com/groups/Tamarknibye